HEARTFELT MOMENTS

A 25 DAY DEVOTIONAL OF SERENITY ON PURPOSE

PAMELA TOWNSEND

Edited by
NICOLE QUEEN

VISION PUBLISHING
—— HOUSE ——

ISBN: 979-8-9933667-8-4
LCCN: 2026903638

Vision Publishing House
support@vision-publishinghouse.com
www.vision-publishinghouse.com

CONTENTS

PREFACE

These writings were birthed many years ago, directly from my intimacy with the Lord. As He spoke quietly to me through nature, inner impressions, and visions, I was careful to document the results of each encounter. So, I filed them away in a folder. Months later, I realized that the season to share the joys of my personal encounters with the Lord had arrived. I knew that my obedience would honor God and be a blessing to the Body of Christ. All honor and glory to God my Father, Jesus my Lord, and the Holy Spirit who equips us for every good work in the earth!

ENABLE YOUR HEART TO SOAR

Hummingbirds are spirit birds. They look fragile, but are very resilient. They can suddenly change course or direction, lift negativity, and respond swiftly. Hummingbirds can travel long distances without being tired; they are independent and present. The beauty of their wisdom is bound to draw you in.

And do not be conformed to this world, but be transformed by the renewing of your mind, that you may prove what is that good and acceptable and perfect will of God.

— ROMANS 12:2 NKJV

But those who wait on the Lord Shall renew their strength; they shall mount up with wings like eagles, They shall run and not be weary, They shall walk and not faint.

— ISAIAH 40:31 NKJV

Meditation Word

met·a·mor·pho·sis (/ˌmedəˈmôrfəsəs/) : a process that
leads to an outward change of the mind, body and
soul for Christ Jesus

Prayer

Heavenly Father, thank You for the process, as we allow You to
transform us from the inside out. Help us not to succumb to our own
thoughts and patterns that we have been subjected to. In Jesus Christ's
Name, we pray. Amen.

Meditate & Journal

EQUIPPED FOR THE BATTLE

*W*e are mighty and powerful in God. We have the ability and strength through the Holy Spirit to conquer every obstacle we face. He will show us how to daily put on the armor, and keep it on. He will whisper who needs prayer and how to pray. He will stand beside us and work through us. Because He is mighty, so are we. We have been forgiven, set apart, loved, never forsaken, and worthy because Jehovah Jireh, our provider, has completed the work.

Finally, my brethren, be strong in the Lord and in the power of his might.

— EPHESIANS 6:10 NKJV

Yet in all these things we are more than conquerors through him who loved us.

— ROMANS 8:37 NKJV

Meditation Word

ar·mor (/ˈärmər/) : equipment needed to be fully armed
    in warfare, including defensive and offensive
    weapons for the battlefield

Prayer

Father God, help us to be strong and mighty on the battlefield of life.
Help us to be fully equipped to handle every situation that arises. In
Jesus Christ's Name, we pray. Amen.

Meditate & Journal

HOPE AND PEACE IN EMMANUEL

As we enter our most secret place, expect to encounter God's peace and hope for each new day. Emmanuel speaks through a whisper or a sweet aroma that enters the room— or into the inner core of who we are.

> This hope we have as an anchor of the soul, both sure and
>   steadfast, and which enters the Presence behind the veil.
>
> — HEBREWS 6:19 NKJV

> For I know the thoughts that I think toward you, says the
>   Lord, thoughts of peace and not of evil, to give you a future
>   and a hope.
>
> —JEREMIAH 29:11 NKJV

Meditation Word

hope *(/hōp/)* : expectation, trust, and confidence; to
anticipate with pleasure because God is with you

Prayer

Help us, Father, to put our confidence and trust in You. No matter
what we face each day, You are trustworthy and we hold onto your
peace. In Jesus Christ's Name, we pray. Amen.

Meditate & Journal

TRUST AND ASSURANCE IN JESUS

*W*e know our present troubles will not last, as we seek God's guidance through prayer and meditation. We will trust and see His mighty hand working in our day-to-day journey here on the earth. He gives us the freedom and boldness to hold Him dear to our hearts and minds with unwavering assurance.

> *Now this is the confidence that we have in him, that if we ask anything according to his will he hears us. And if we know that he hears us, whatever we ask, we know that we have the petitions that we have asked of him.*
>
> — 1 JOHN 5:14-15 NKJV

> *Oh, taste and see that the Lord is good. Blessed is the man who trusts in him!*
>
> — PSALM 34:8 NKJV

Meditation Word

*con·fi·dence (/ˈkänfəd(ə)ns/) : courage, boldness to speak
freely, unhindered assurance*

Prayer

Heavenly Father, cultivate in us a spirit of boldness when needed and help us believe in our hearts Your promises are 'yes' and 'amen.' In Jesus Christ's Name, we pray. Amen.

* * *

Meditate & Journal

DELIGHT IN THE LORD

*W*e choose to put on joy and delight within because we were created after your likeness. Thank You for helping us find the treasures deep within our being to show the world that You are a loving Savior.

> *Fear not, for I am with you: Be not dismayed, For I am Your*
> *God. I will strengthen you. Yes, I will help you. I will*
> *uphold you with my righteous right hand.*
>
> — ISAIAH 41:10 NKJV

> *You will show me the path of life: In your presence is fullness*
> *of joy: At your right hand are pleasures forevermore.*
>
> — PSALM 16:11 NKJV

Meditation Word

joy *(/joi/)* : rejoicing, delight, gladness knowing that our
Lord and Savior is always with us.

Prayer

Father God, help us to be still and wait upon You to strengthen and
fill us with Your power and assurance. Your way is better than silver
and gold. In Jesus Christ's Name, we pray. Amen.

* * *

Meditate & Journal

GLORY IN HIS PRESENCE

*A*s the seasons change and the trees bring forth their leaves, God commands heaven to open and sprinkle rain— making dark limbs vibrate light to reflect its glorious color. Let us ponder on the goodness of God and open our hearts to the brilliant colors and fragrances surrounding us each day. May we be a sweet fragrance for someone today!

> *The heavens declare the glory of God: And the firmament*
> *shows his handiwork.*
>
> — PSALM 19:1 NKJV

> *But thanks be to God, who is Christ always leads us in*
> *triumphal procession, and through us spreads the*
> *fragrance of the knowledge of him everywhere.*
>
> — 2 CORINTHIANS 2:14 NKJV

Meditation Word

fra·grance (/ˈfrāgrəns/) : aroma; sweet; good smell;
  comfort to the soul, as we allow Jesus to be first place
  in all we say and do

Prayer

Father, come surround us with Your sweet Glory, and may we in return give off that same sweetness to those we encounter today. In Jesus Christ's Name, we pray. Amen.

Meditate & Journal

FREEDOM IN THE RELEASE

*W*hen we seem detached from life, our minds may wonder what's happening. How can I find a sense of peace in the midst of confusion and frustration? Who am I and what is my purpose in pain? Where can we go and who can help us find the answers to life's unexplainable questions? The answer is *Jesus*!

We can find hope, peace, joy, restoration, and answers to life's questions that are only found in the Word of God. When we don't know what to say or how to pray, we can call on the Name of Jesus. It's not about eloquent words or speech, it's about our love for each other, despite our faults and confusion. Jesus is our living example. When the world says you can't, the Word says you can!

> *Therefore, since we are surrounded by so great a cloud of*
> *witnesses, let us also lay aside every weight, and sin which*
> *so easily ensnares us, and let us run with endurance the*
> *race that is set before us, looking unto Jesus, the author*
> *and finisher of our faith, who for the joy that was set*

before Him endured the cross, despising the shame, and has sat down at the right hand of the throne of God.

— HEBREWS 12:1-2 NKJV

Greater love has no one than this, than to lay down one's life for his friends.

— JOHN 15:13 NKJV

Meditation Word

love *(/ləv/)* : pure, willful, sacrificial love; unconditional love; this is the love of the Father we encounter every minute of the day

Prayer

Gracious Heavenly Father, help us to draw close to You. May we endure our earthly race with love, patience, and kindness toward all we come in contact with— each and every day. In Jesus Christ's Name, we pray. Amen.

Meditate & Journal

_____
_____
_____
_____
_____
_____
_____
_____
_____
_____
_____
_____
_____
_____
_____
_____
_____
_____
_____
_____
_____
_____
_____
_____
_____
_____
_____
_____
_____
_____
_____
_____

PROMISE IN THE RAIN

When a storm erupts and the trees blow from one side to another, who will comfort your children's hearts, hear their cry, or capture their tears? His name is *Love*— the One who was and is to come! He is coming quickly to set everything in order. Keep believing and trusting in the One who created all hearts. He sends the latter rain, and in due season, we shall weep no more.

> *But the Helper, the Holy Spirit, whom the Father will send in My name, He will teach you all things, and bring to your remembrance all things that I said to you. Peace I leave with you, My peace I give to you: not as the world gives do I give to you. Let not your heart be troubled, neither let it be afraid.* — JOHN 15:26-27 *NKJV*

> *Let the peoples praise You, O God: Let all the peoples praise You. Then the earth shall yield her increase: God, our own God, shall bless us.* — PSALM 67:5-6 *NKJV*

Meditation Word

in·crease (/in'krēs/) : to grow, mature, heighten aware-
ness that we are not left alone on this journey; we
shall bless the Lord all the time

Prayer

Thank You, Father, for sending us the Comforter— the Holy Spirit—
to remind us that He is ever-present, especially when we cry out to
You. Help us gain a greater understanding that we are not alone, and
that increase is a promise. In Jesus Christ's Name, we pray. Amen.

Meditate & Journal

CONNECTED TO THE CREATOR

*E*ven the leaves need to stay connected to the vine for nourishment. They start out small and light green. When the heavens open up and drop rain upon the leaf, it begins to take flight and expand. The process is slow, but with each raindrop gently soaking into the cracks, the leaf grows and becomes radiant, over-shadowing its children with love.

> *If you abide in Me, and My words abide in you, you will ask*
> *what you desire, and it shall be done for you.*
>
> — JOHN 15:7 NKJV

> *Meditate on these things, give yourself entirely to them, that*
> *your progress may be evident to all.*
>
> — 1 TIMOTHY 4:15 NKJV

Meditation Word

a·bide (/əbīd/) : to reside; to live; to remain, stay
connected to Christ Jesus

Prayer

Father God, help us stay alert and remain in the light of Your
countenance. In Jesus Christ's Name, we pray. Amen.

* * *

Meditate & Journal

_____
_____
_____
_____
_____
_____
_____
_____
_____
_____
_____
_____
_____
_____
_____
_____
_____
_____
_____
_____
_____
_____
_____
_____
_____
_____
_____
_____
_____
_____
_____
_____

OBEDIENCE EQUALS BLESSING

*A*s I sit and watch the birds quarrel over a house built in the tree, one stands at the entrance, guarding its place of residence. Others try to force their way in by attacking with fear and intimidation. The one guarding his house stands strong and fights the attacks of the other birds trying to make their way in.

This proves that we can defend and stand strong in the midst of attacks and trials. We protect what we love. So we must stand strong, guard our house against the tempter, and not allow him to come in to take up residence. God has given us a spiritual house, a holy temple where He dwells, as a living sanctuary acceptable in His sight. Let us not forget we have the weapons of warfare to trample on all the power of the evil one.

Behold, I stand at the door and knock. If anyone hears my voice and opens the door. I will come in to him and dine with him, and he with me.

— REVELATION 3:20 NKJV

For the weapons of our warfare are not carnal but mighty in God for pulling down strongholds, casting down arguments and every high thing that exalts itself against the knowledge of God, bringing every thought into captivity to the obedience of Christ, and being ready to punish all disobedience when your obedience is fulfilled.

— 2 CORINTHIANS 10:4-6 NKJV

Meditation Word

stand (/stand/) : you remain firm, immovable, and fixed; keep your eyes on Jesus

Prayer

Father, our heart's cry is cast upon You. May You find our spiritual house solid, as the rock of our present and eternal salvation. In Jesus Christ's Name, we pray. Amen.

* * *

Meditate & Journal

UNCONDITIONAL LOVE

*J*esus, we know in the light of Your countenance and assurance through Your Word, that You have molded and created us to be a loving living example to others. We are filled with Your glory to illuminate others to encounter Your love.

Your word is a lamp to my feet and a light to my path.

— 2 CORINTHIANS 10:4-6 NKJV

For I am persuaded that neither death nor life, nor angels nor principalities nor powers, nor things present nor things to come, nor height nor depth, nor any other created thing, shall be able to separate us from the love of God which is in Christ Jesus our Lord.

— ROMANS 8:38-39 NKJV

Meditation Word

light (/līt/) : God's word is illuminated, as we read the
Scriptures; Jesus promises to direct our steps

Prayer

Father God, answer us speedily to know You are for us and not
against us. Help us to combat the battlefield of the mind and comprehend that nothing can separate us from Your love. In Jesus Christ's
Name, we pray. Amen.

* * *

Meditate & Journal

PRAYER IS THE FATHER'S HEART

The love of God has been shed abroad in every living creature made and orchestrated by Him. His hand is sovereign and mighty. Therefore, whom shall I fear? He knows every hurt, fear, and desire. My soul cries out for the living God. Deep places that scream out are comforted with His peace. He calms my soul that mourns within me. He bends His ear to hear every Word from His holy throne and catches my tears. As He sits next to the Father, making intercession on my behalf, He releases ministering angels to encamp and surround me with a shield saying, "Do not be dismayed, for I AM God almighty who was and is and is to come."

Now hope does not disappoint, because the love of God has been poured out in our hearts by the Holy Spirit who was given to us.

— ROMANS 5:5 NKJV

> *Who is he who condemns? It is Christ who died, and further-*
> *more is also risen, who is even at the right hand of God,*
> *who also makes intercession for us.*

— ROMANS: 8:34 NKJV

Meditation Word

in·ter·ces·sion (/ˌin(t)ərˈseSH(ə)n/) : stepping in the gap
and praying for our family members, co-workers,
neighbors, friends, the nation, and our country

Prayer

Father, we move all hindrances of our hearts out of the way. We lay
ourselves at your feet for those in need. In Jesus Christ's Name, we
pray. Amen.

* * *

Meditate & Journal

POWER IN PRAISE

*W*here does my help come from? My help cometh from the Lord who is all powerful and mighty in the land. He gives power to the weak and builds character in his children. As John the Baptist conveyed, we must decrease and allow God's spirit to increase within us. As we walk in the land of the living, there's no time to question the unknown. We must trust God to show us the way to everlasting love, comfort, joy, and peace. His name is above every name; He gives breath to every creature on the earth to bring glory to His name. Emanuel is His name— God with us. He is Jehovah Shalom, the God of Peace.

> *I will lift up my eyes to the hills- From whence comes my help?*
> *My help comes from the Lord, Who made heaven and*
> *earth.*
>
> — PSALM 121:1-2 NKJV

Be strong and of good courage, do not fear nor be afraid of them: for the Lord your God, He is the One who goes with you. He will not leave you nor forsake you.

— DEUTERONOMY 31:6 NKJV

Meditation Word

help (*/help/*) : we seek the Lord and lift our heads and praise Him before the answer is provided; trust and confidence in our Lord and Savior

Prayer

Father God, as we seek Your face and not Your hand, help us to be character builders for Your kingdom here on the earth. We will praise you in the process. In Jesus Christ's Name, we pray. Amen.

* * *

Meditate & Journal

LIGHT OVERCOMES DARKNESS

*H*e was sent by God and born of a virgin woman in a stable to humble and obedient parents. They loved the Son who would eventually expose the darkness in the hearts of all creation. John the Baptist testified of this light and spoke the Word to the Jews to repent, and expose their true human nature. He was not the true Messiah, but spoke of the One which was to come— the true light, hope of glory, and God of all creation and love!

> *Your eyes saw my substance, being yet unformed. And in your book they were all written, the days fashioned for me, When as yet there was none of them.*
>
> — PSALM 139:16 NKJV

> *Then Jesus spoke to them again saying, I am the light of the world. He who follows Me shall not walk in darkness, but have the light of life.*
>
> — JOHN 8:12 NKJV

Meditation Word

re·veal *(/rə'vēl/)* : God is making known to us the beauty
of his holiness before we were formed in our moth-
er's womb

Prayer

Righteous Judge and Father, thank You that we do not walk as those
without the light. We allow the Holy Spirit to permeate our souls to
speak the truth about our true identity. In Jesus Christ's Name, we
pray. Amen.

Meditate & Journal

EXCHANGE DOUBT
TO RESTORATION

*T*he winds blow, but where do they come from? We can't see it but we feel its coolness or warmth shouting from God's throne room, speaking unto our hearts. Although we cannot physically see God, we can feel and sense His presence. We can trust Him to take one more step and climb one more mountain. As the elevation gets more intense, so does our walk with God in Christ Jesus. Deeper and deeper, we draw from the well of love and living water. It cleanses and purifies us into a living epistle, rooted and grounded, being prepared to meet the King of Kings and Lord of Lords.

> *The wind blows where it wishes, and you hear the sound of it,*
> *but cannot tell where it comes from and where it goes. So is*
> *everyone who is born of the Spirit.* — JOHN 3:8 NKJV

> *Let us draw near with a true heart in full assurance of faith,*
> *having our hearts sprinkled from an evil conscience and*
> *our bodies washed with pure water.* — HEBREWS
> 10:22 NKJV

Meditation Word

wind (*/wind/*) : we cannot see the wind, but we feel and
sense the changes happening internally that create an
external reward, as we draw near Jesus

Prayer

Father, we chose to draw near Your rivers of living water. Come
refresh and restore us with wholeness, and a pure heart for You and
Your creation. In Jesus Christ's Name, we pray. Amen.

* * *

Meditate & Journal

BEAUTY IN THE ROUTINE

*a*s the sun shines down and heats the earth, rays reflect beauty and glory. Flowers start to spring up from a long cold winter, giving birth to radiant color and fragrance that pierces the air. He gives us a glimpse of His splendor and glory. As we try to comprehend the depth, width, and length of His creativity, we seek Him alone to open our eyes to the beauty surrounding us.

> *O Lord, how manifold are Your works! In wisdom You have made this all.*
>
> — PSALM 104:24 NKJV

> *So then neither he who plants is anything, nor he who waters, but God who gives the increase.*
>
> — 1 CORINTHIANS 3:7 NKJV

Meditation Word

wis·dom (/ˈwizdəm/) : we make time to encounter the
    Lord to help guide us through every decision to
    know Him and understand His ways for our lives
    and eternal reward

Prayer

Father God, open our spiritual eyes to see the splendor and glory
surrounding us each day, as we venture into our workplace for Your
glory. In Jesus Christ's Name, we pray. Amen.

Meditate & Journal

FREE TO BE ME

I pondered in my mind: How can I break free from the thoughts running through my mind? How can I achieve my heart's desires feeling empty and alone? The answer came when the Word washed over my entire being. I must run after Jesus with an open invitation and heart, yearning to be filled with His manifested glory and peace to be me.

> *Where can I go from your spirit? Or where can I flee from*
> *your presence? If I ascend into heaven you are there: if I*
> *make my bed in hell behold, You are there. If I take the*
> *wings of the morning, and dwell in the uttermost parts of*
> *the sea, Even there your hand shall lead me, and your right*
> *hand shall hold me.*
>
> — PSALM 139:7-10 NKJV

> *Ask, and it will be given to you, seek, and you will find: knock,*
> *and it will be opened to you.*
>
> — MATTHEW 7:7 NKJV

Meditation Word

seek *(/sēk/)* : we find time in the light of what we love
and cherish; Jesus will always be listening and
providing the way with each and every season

Prayer

Father, we shall not flee from You, but run towards You with open
hearts and minds to seek Your counsel in each season. Remind us in
our daily walks and talks with You that we are loved and cherished. In
Jesus Christ's Name, we pray. Amen.

* * *

Meditate & Journal

PRAISE TO THE KING OF GLORY

*G*od is our redeemer, rock, and fortress in times of need. Our God is a mighty powerful, everlasting Prince of Peace. There is no other God like our God. He saves, heals, and sets the captives free. Where can we flee from His presence? He is our hope and takes no part in perverse ways. He's patient and loving, and always stands at the door waiting for his children's hearts to open and receive Him. It's the Father's good pleasure to give His children His peace. Although we may not understand all of God's ways, we must believe and trust Him, as we walk as Children of Light in the countenance of His presence, one day at a time.

> *For unto us a Child is born; unto us a Son is given; and the government will be upon his shoulder; And his name will be called Wonderful, Counselor, Mighty God, Everlasting Father, Prince of Peace.*
>
> — ISAIAH 9:6 NKJV

The Lord is merciful and gracious, Slow to anger, and
abounding in mercy.

— PSALM 103:8 NKJV

Meditation Word

peace (/pēs/) : freedom exists after consulting
Emmanuel God with us and we can rest in that
knowing.

Prayer

Jesus, You came down from a heavenly kingdom to dwell with man and expose the darkness within our hearts. Help us, dear Lord, to discern motives and provide us with Your rest and peace. In Jesus Christ's Name, we pray. Amen.

* * *

Meditate & Journal

BEAUTY AS YOU GROW

*W*e are trees planted by living waters. As the sun shines on the tree and is nourished by water, so do the roots grow with each passing day. Before you know it, a soft bud appears. As it opens up, colors appear. It's radiant and beautiful, as it grows and feeds by the Father's love— springing up with new life and abundant glory for all the world to see and enjoy!

> *He shall be like a tree Planted by the rivers of living water.*
> *That brings forth its fruit in its season. Whose leaf also*
> *shall not wither And whatever he does shall prosper.*
>
> — PSALM 1:3 NKJV

> *Let the sea roar, and all its fullness: let the field rejoice, and all*
> *that is in it. Then the trees of the woods shall rejoice before*
> *the Lord. For he is coming to judge the earth. Oh, give*
> *thanks to the Lord, for he is good! For His mercy endures*
> *forever.*
>
> —1 CHRONICLES 16:32-34 NKJV

Meditation Word

wa·ter (/ˈwôdər) : staying connected to Jesus is flowing
    nourishment; a quench-refiller of His life-giving
    substance

Prayer

Father God, You said when we stay connected to the living water,
which is Your Word, we shall flourish and spring up with new life.
Help us to bear fruit so that You may receive all the Glory. In Jesus
Christ's Name, we pray. Amen.

* * *

Meditate & Journal

INABILITY TO ABILITY

*W*e are mighty and powerful women. We have the ability and strength through the Holy Spirit to conquer every obstacle we face. He will show us how to daily put on the armor, and keep it on. He will whisper to us who needs prayer and instruct us on how to pray. He will stand beside us and work through us. And because He is mighty, so are we. We have been forgiven, set apart, loved, never forsaken, and worthy, all because Jesus our provider completed the finished work.

> *Finally, my brethren, be strong in the Lord and in the power of his might. Put on the whole armor of God, that you may be able to stand against the wiles of the devil.*
>
> — EPHESIANS 6:10-11 NKJV

> *Be strong and of good courage, do not fear nor be afraid of them: for the Lord your God, He is the One who goes with you. He will not leave you nor forsake you.*
>
> — DEUTERONOMY 31:6 NKJV

Meditation Word

a·bil·i·ty *(/əˈbiləd ē/)* : our gifts are multiplied when we
surrender our capacity and seek the one who can
exceed beyond comprehension

Prayer

Father God, help us to kneel at the foot of the Cross and surrender
our mindset cultivated by the world's standards. Guide us on how to
put on the armor and keep it on. Help us to be confident and trust in
You. In Jesus Christ's Name, we pray. Amen.

Meditate & Journal

EXTENSION OF LIGHT

*W*hen I reflect on Your ways from the beginning of time, and think about every plot and plan that attempted to obstruct any good in our journey with You, You have always found a way to make the crooked path straight for us. You always shine the light when it seems the darkest.

> *Every valley shall be exalted and every mountain and hill brought low: The crooked places shall be made straight and the rough places smooth.*
>
> — ISAIAH 40:4 NKJV

> *Your word is a lamp to my feet and a Light to my path.*
>
> — PSALM 119:105 NKJV

Meditation Word

in·ter·ven·tion (/ˌin(t)ərˈven(t)SH(ə)n/) : *to help guide the course for a particular condition in order to prevent a certain outcome*

Prayer

Father God, we are in desperate need of Your intervention. We cry out and ask for Your mercy and grace to be extended upon us. Turn the hearts of Your children back to You. Flood us with Your presence, open up our spiritual eyes to taste and see that Your love endures forever. Fill our hearts with more of You and let wisdom enter in. In Jesus Christ's Name, we pray. Amen.

* * *

Meditate & Journal

COMMIT TO THE CALL

*F*ather, Your Word states that when we don't know what to say or how to pray, we can call on the Name of Jesus. It's not about eloquent words or speech; it's about the love we have for each other through seeking and searching for You as our living example. When the world says you can't, the Word says you can.

I can do all things through Christ who strengthens me.

— PHILIPPIANS 4:11 NKJV

For to this you were called because Christ also suffered for us, leaving us an example, that you should follow His steps: Who committed no sin, Nor was deceit found in His mouth.

—1 PETER 2:21-22 NKJV

Meditation Word

com·mit (/kə'mit/) : the act of engaging in a promise to
do something; to make a decision to trust or
give over

Prayer

Father, help us to actively and willingly put our faith in You.
Strengthen us to walk out this journey with You. Do not let us grow
weary and lost in this deserted land called life. We seek your holy
presence and ask You to help us commit to following in Your foot-
steps. In Jesus Christ's Name, we pray. Amen.

* * *

Meditate & Journal

WEEP NO MORE

When a storm erupts and the trees blow from one side to another, who will comfort Your children's hearts, hear their cries, or capture their tears? His name is Love, the One who was and is to come. He is coming quickly to set everything in order. Keep believing and trusting in the One who created all hearts. He sends the latter rain, and in due season, we shall weep no more.

> *You number my wanderings: Put my tears into Your bottle:*
> *Are they not in Your book?*
>
> — PSALM 56:8 NKJV

> *Those who sow in tears shall reap in joy.*
>
> — PSALM 126:5 NKJV

Meditation Word

cap·ture (/ˈkap(t)SHər/) : an act or instance of obtaining,
such as winning or gaining over adversity

Prayer

Father, we thank You for every tear that falls from our eyes that You
see and capture. Bring back to our remembrance, by the power of
your Holy Spirit, when we are going through adversity and trials that
You are here for us. Help us to remember that You are good and will
turn our sorrow into dancing. In Jesus Christ's Name, we pray. Amen.

* * *

Meditate & Journal

STAY CONNECTED TO THE VINE

I am a tree standing upright before my God. The higher the level, the deeper the roots grow and expand. Staying connected means being nourished and fed by the Father. He's the provider and Prince of Peace. Nothing is too hard for Him; no question is impossible to answer. His help is always available to those who abide in Him and allow His spirit to abide in them. Our Father speaks truth in His Word to all generations— past, present, and future. God will elevate our children, bring them to higher ground, and expand our territory to conquer hills, plains, and valleys, as we stay connected to our Savior.

> *I am the vine, you are the branches, He who abides in Me, and*
> *I in him, bears much fruit for without Me you can do*
> *nothing.*
>
> — JOHN 15:5 NKJV

He shall be like a tree planted by the rivers of water, that bring
forth its fruit in its season, whose leaf also shall not wither:
And whatever he does shall prosper.

— PSALM 1:3 NKJV

Meditation Word

vine (/v ῑn/) : something that produces and multiplies, as
the Father prunes off the necessary impurities within
for the outward manifestation to appear

Prayer:

Dear Heavenly Father, help us to stay connected and flow with the
rhythms of Your Word, as we meditate. Remove all distractions and
dysfunction among us. Help us to remove all worry, doubt, and fear
within, so we can help others in need, stand upright, and reflect Your
glory to others. In Jesus Christ's Name, we pray. Amen.

* * *

Meditate & Journal

_____
_____
_____
_____
_____
_____
_____
_____
_____
_____
_____
_____
_____
_____
_____
_____
_____
_____
_____
_____
_____
_____
_____
_____
_____
_____
_____
_____
_____
_____
_____
_____
_____
_____

THIRSTY FOR REVIVAL

*A*s the deer pants for the water brook, so do our hearts thirst for the living God. Renewed water springs up and out when our soul is downcast. He quenches our thirst with one touch of the Master's Hand. He leads us beside the still waters. And with loving arms, He restores His children. He places them back on His holy mountain— shining brightly, while taking delight in each one.

> *The Lord is my shepherd I shall not want. He makes me to lie down in green pastures: He leads me beside the still waters. He restores my soul. He leads me in the paths of right-eousness for His name's sake.*
>
> — PSALM 23:1-3 NKJV

> *Our soul waits for the Lord: He is our help and our shield. For our heart shall rejoice in Him, Because we have trusted in His holy name, Let You mercy, O Lord, be upon us. Just as we hope in you.*
>
> — PSALM 33:20-22 NKJV

Meditation Word

re·new (/rə'no͞o/) : *when the Lord revives us (removing the hurt, pain, disappointments, rejection, and failures) back to our intended path*

Prayer

Lord Jesus, thank You in advance for providing a way of escape, as we wait and meditate on Your words. As we rejoice in You, we ask for Your instructions and guidance to lead us and restore our minds from past wounds. In Jesus Christ's Name, we pray. Amen.

* * *

Meditate & Journal

AN INVITATION TO
KNOW JESUS CHRIST

If you have been reading these daily devotionals and sense a stirring in your heart (a longing for peace, forgiveness, or a deeper relationship with God), know that this is the gentle invitation of the Holy Spirit drawing you to Jesus Christ.

The Bible tells us:

> *"If you confess with your mouth the Lord Jesus and believe in your heart that God has raised Him from the dead, you will be saved. For with the heart one believes unto righteousness, and with the mouth confession is made unto salvation."*

> — ROMANS 10:9–10

Salvation is not about being perfect or having all the answers. It is about believing in *Jesus Christ, the Son of God*, who died on the cross for our sins and rose again so that we might have new life. So, if you desire to receive Jesus as your Lord and Savior, you can begin by praying this simple prayer (on the following page) from your heart.

Lord Jesus,

I confess that I am a sinner in need of Your grace.
I believe in my heart that You died on the cross for all of my sins and
that You rose again so that I may have eternal life.
I confess with my mouth that Jesus Christ is Lord.

Today, I repent of my sins and turn my heart fully toward You,
and invite You into my heart and my life.
Be my Lord, my Savior, and my Redeemer.

Thank You for loving me, forgiving me,
and giving me new life in You.

I receive Your salvation by faith.
In Jesus' name, Amen.

* * *

If you prayed this prayer sincerely, know that you are now a Child of God. Begin nurturing your relationship with Him by reading the Word of God, spending time in prayer, and connecting with a Bible-believing church community where you can grow in faith and fellowship.

May this be the beginning of a beautiful journey with Jesus—one marked by grace, truth, healing, and everlasting hope.

ACKNOWLEDGMENTS

First and foremost, I give all glory and honor to God. I thank Him for placing this gift within me and entrusting me to share it with others for encouragement, hope, and healing. None of this would be possible without His presence, guidance, and faithfulness.

I would like to thank my leaders, mentors, family, and friends for their prayers, support, and encouragement—especially for pushing me to complete this book when the journey felt long. Your support has meant more to me than words can express.

Thank you to everyone who has poured into my life along this journey. May this book be a reflection of God's love and a blessing to all who encounter it.

ABOUT THE AUTHOR

Pamela Townsend is a licensed and ordained minister of the Gospel of Jesus Christ. She is passionate about saving souls, discipleship, and seeing God's Word manifested, to bring hope and healing to God's creation.

www.ingramcontent.com/pod-product-compliance
Lightning Source LLC
Chambersburg PA
CBHW050444150626
46551CB00028B/1305